To C.B. and all the bugs, blooms,
and beasts that inspired this book.

Copyright © 2009 by Bob Barner.
All rights reserved.

Book design by Amy E. Achaibou.
Typeset in Iconified and Toronto Subway.
The illustrations in this book were rendered in paper collage.
Manufactured in Singapore.

Library of Congress Cataloging-in-Publication Data
Barner, Bob.
  Dinosaurs roar, butterflies soar! / by Bob Barner.
     p. cm.
  ISBN 978-0-8118-5663-8
  1. Butterflies, Fossil—Juvenile literature. I. Title.
  QE832.L5B37 2009
  565'.78—dc22
  2008016783

10 9 8 7 6 5 4 3 2 1

Chronicle Books LLC
680 Second Street, San Francisco, California 94107

www.chroniclekids.com

Dinosaurs ROAR, Butterflies SOAR!

By Bob Barner

chronicle books · san francisco

Millions and millions of years ago,
tiny new creatures fluttered
into the dinosaurs' world
and changed it
FOREVER.

Dinosaurs first appeared on Earth 248 million years ago. Most were herbivores that roamed from field to field in search of food.

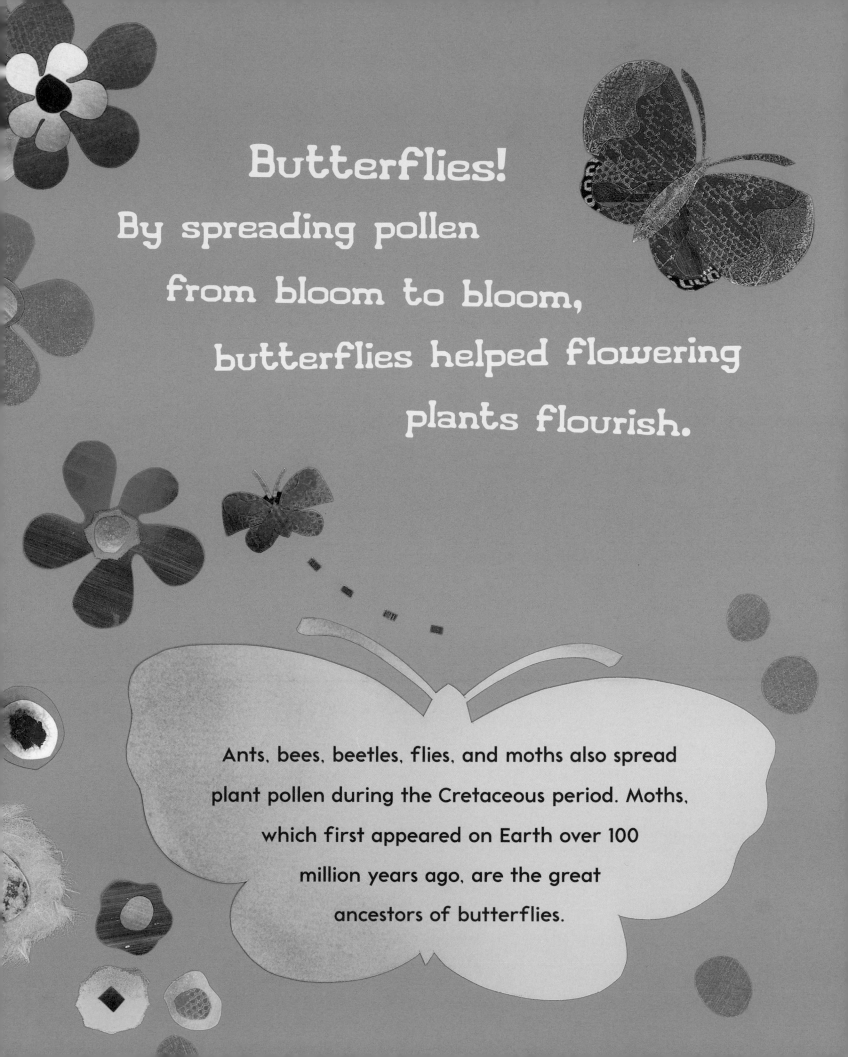

Butterflies!
By spreading pollen
from bloom to bloom,
butterflies helped flowering
plants flourish.

Ants, bees, beetles, flies, and moths also spread plant pollen during the Cretaceous period. Moths, which first appeared on Earth over 100 million years ago, are the great ancestors of butterflies.

Flowering plants made more air
for dinosaurs to breathe and huge
amounts of food for them to eat.

Dinosaurs were accidental farmers that helped plants grow. As they walked, their feet opened the soil, and their droppings fertilized seeds that grew into new plants.

Never before had so many different kinds of plants and animals lived together on Earth.

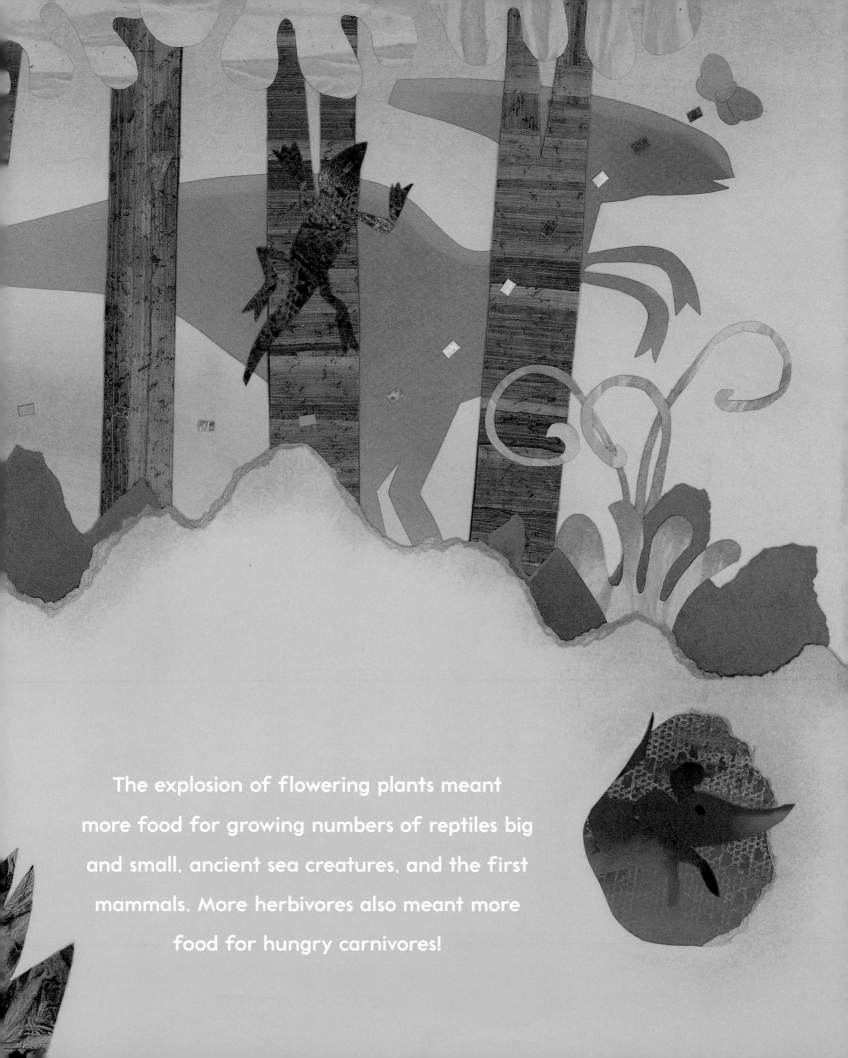

The explosion of flowering plants meant
more food for growing numbers of reptiles big
and small, ancient sea creatures, and the first
mammals. More herbivores also meant more
food for hungry carnivores!

Dinosaurs and ancient butterflies
lived together for millions
of years . . .

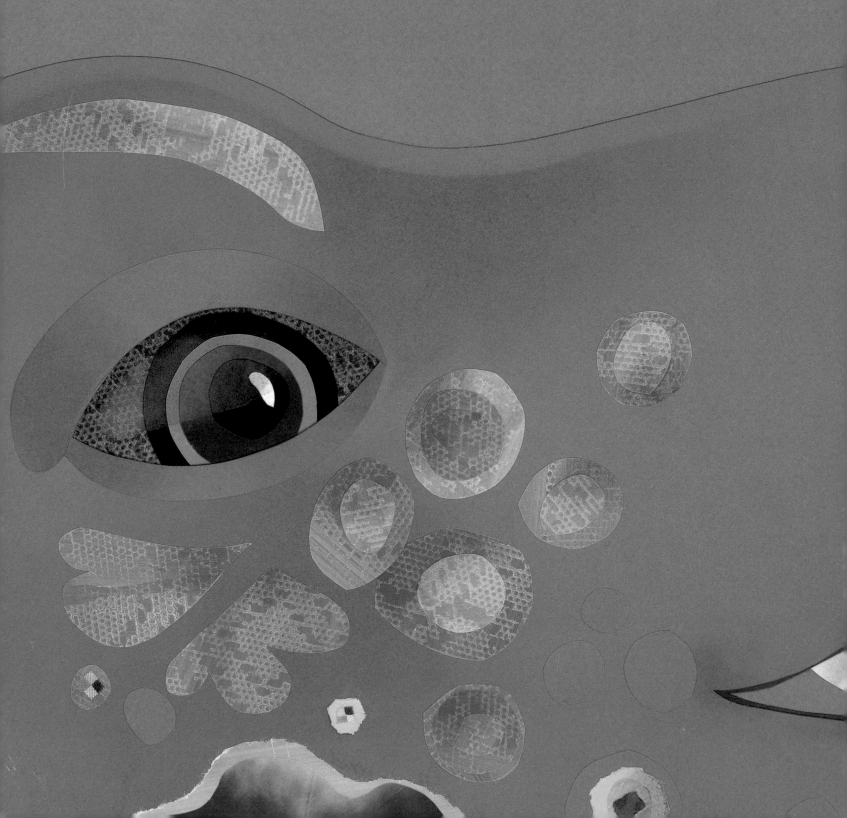

until, suddenly,
their time together
ended.

A huge asteroid CRASHED into Earth, forming clouds of steam and dust that blocked the sun.

In addition to the 6-mile-wide asteroid that plummeted to Earth, fiery volcanic eruptions may have filled the sky with a thick layer of smoke and ash.

Without heat and light from the sun, many plants could not grow. Dinosaurs didn't have enough food to eat and they soon became EXTINCT.

When the herbivores were gone, so was the food for the carnivores. Some scientists think that the cooling of the planet and the spread of disease may have also led to the dinosaur extinction.

But, butterflies
lived!

They were small and
found just enough
nectar to drink and
air to breathe.

Insects, plants, small mammals, and reptiles
didn't need as much food as the dinosaurs.
This made it possible for many of
them to survive.

KENNEDY

Over the next 65 million years, butterflies fluttered past saber-toothed cats, woolly mammoths, and the first humans.

The butterflies we see today are very similar in size and shape to the prehistoric ones. As with dinosaurs, no one knows the colors of these ancient creatures. Over 200,000 kinds of moths and 18,000 kinds of butterflies live on Earth today.

So, the next time you see a fluttering butterfly or smell a flower, remember that millions of years ago a T. rex may have done the same.

Many plant, butterfly, and dinosaur secrets remain hidden in fossils and rocks waiting to be found, maybe by you.

DAYS OF THE DINOSAURS

FIRST DINOSAURS

FIRST FLOWERS AND FIRST BUTTERFLIES

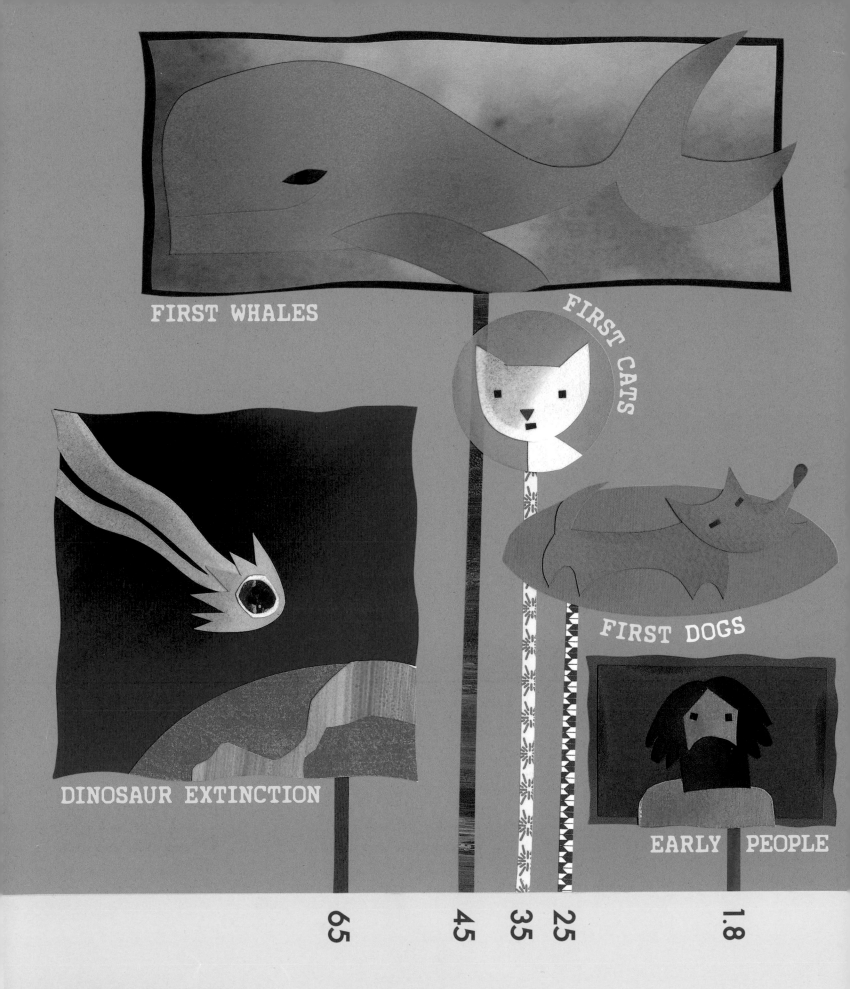

FIRST WHALES

FIRST CATS

FIRST DOGS

DINOSAUR EXTINCTION

EARLY PEOPLE

65   45   35   25   1.8

YEARS AGO

Big Birds

Pterosaurs, with wings 40 feet wide, lived at the time of the dinosaurs. They were not dinosaurs but giant flying reptiles.

Fancy Feathers

Scientists believe that some dinosaurs had feathers. They recently discovered the fossil of a baby T. rex with feathers. Scientists believe that the feathers helped keep the young Tyrannosaurus warm and may have fallen out as it got older.

Dinosaur Mom

The dinosaur Maiasaura scooped out a nest 7 feet wide to hold the 25 grapefruit-sized eggs it laid. They were carefully arranged in circles and covered with vegetation to keep them warm until they hatched.

Dangerous Diet

Sowing Seeds

A plant starts as a seed. The seed sprouts and grows into a plant. The mature plant produces seeds to start the cycle of life again.

Eager Eaters

Caterpillars spend much of their time eating, until they form a chrysalis and wait to be born as a butterfly.

Bunches of Bugs

Insects make up 80 percent of all creatures on Earth. More than one million kinds of insects have been discovered so far. Insects eat 20 percent of Earth's vegetation each year.

Some caterpillars eat the leaves of poisonous plants but are not harmed. When these caterpillars become butterflies, their colorful wings are a signal to predators that eating them is a very bad idea.